PIVOTAL

CREATIVE ● EDUCATION

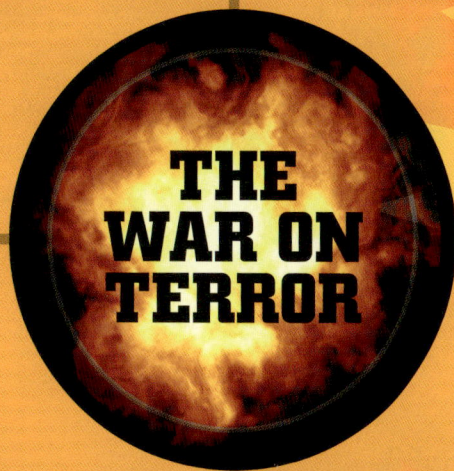

THE WAR ON TERROR

BY JESSICA GUNDERSON

MOMENTS

Published by Creative Education
P.O. Box 227, Mankato, Minnesota 56002
Creative Education is an imprint of The Creative Company
www.thecreativecompany.us

Design and production by The Design Lab
Art direction by Rita Marshall
Printed by Corporate Graphics in the United States of America

Photographs by Alamy (Acbag, Aurora Photos, Peter Jordan),
Corbis (Larry Downing/Reuters, Brownie Harris, Rob Howard),
Getty Images (Ahmad Al-Rubaye/AFP, David Allocca/Timepix/Time
& Life Pictures, Paula Bronstein, Charles Caratini/AFP, CNN,
Eric Draper/White House, Ariel Hermonl/MOD, Stephen Jaffe/
AFP, Peter Macdlarmid, Matt Moyer, Oleg Nikishin, Joe Raedle,
Johannes Simon/AFP, Chung Sung-Jun, Mario Tama, Diana Walker/
Time & Life Pictures, Mark Wilson), iStockphoto (Andrew
Robinson)

Library of Congress Cataloging-in-Publication Data

Gunderson, Jessica.
Pivotal moments / by Jessica Gunderson.
p. cm. — (The war on terror)
Includes bibliographical references and index.
Summary: An examination of landmark events in the ongoing war
against Islamic extremists, spotlighting such incidents as
the 9/11 attacks, the invasion of Iraq, and the creation of
new democracies.
ISBN 978-1-60818-102-5
1. Terrorism—United States—Juvenile literature. 2. War on
Terrorism, 2001-2009—Juvenile literature. 3. Iraq War, 2003—
Juvenile literature. I. Title.

HV6432.G86 2011
909.83'1—dc22   2010033845

CPSIA: 110310 PO1387

First Edition
9 8 7 6 5 4 3 2 1

TABLE OF CONTENTS

President George W. Bush rallies firefighters, police, and other workers amid the rubble of the World Trade Center on September 14, 2001.

I n the late 1980s, a conflict rooted in terrorism began to rear its head on a global scale. This strife pitted Islamic fundamentalists, radical religious **militants** springing primarily from nations in the Middle East, against the countries and culture of the Western world. Spilling across parts of four decades, this conflict—which came to be known from the Western perspective as "The War on Terror"—grew from bombings and guerrilla combat into the first large-scale war of the 21st century, marked by the infamous events of September 11, 2001, and intensive military campaigns in the countries of Afghanistan and Iraq.

The United States—a beacon of Western-style **democracy** and culture—has been a primary target of terrorists in such incidents as the 1983 bombing of military barracks in Beirut, Lebanon, and 1993 and 2001 attacks on the World Trade Center in New York. America's allies, including such nations as Great Britain and Spain, have suffered terrorist attacks as well. These events, and especially the "9/11" attacks, prompted increasingly strong responses by American and allied military forces that became all-out war. As key terrorist leaders continued to evade capture in the years that followed, and as new tensions flared throughout the Middle East, the Western world employed military might, created new legislation, and sought **diplomatic** solutions as it tried to both crush terrorist groups and pave the way toward long-term peace.

CHAPTER ONE

THE RISE OF MODERN TERRORISM

On the morning of October 23, 1983, in Beirut, Lebanon, a yellow truck carrying 12,000 pounds (5,445 kg) of explosives crashed through a barbed-wire fence outside U.S. Marine barracks, zoomed past sentry posts, and then smashed into the lobby of the barracks. Before security personnel could respond, the truck exploded. The detonation collapsed the 4-story building, killing 241 troops and injuring 60 more. Moments later, a second truck bomb exploded near French army barracks about 3.5 miles (6 km) away, killing 58 and injuring 15.

Although the attacks were not aimed at civilians, the U.S. government classified them as terrorist acts and conducted investigations. It quickly became clear that the bombings had been in protest of Western presence in Lebanon, a country in the Middle East that borders Israel. The country was embroiled in a conflict with Israel, which had invaded in 1982 after being attacked by Palestinian forces by way of Lebanon. The U.S. and international allies such as France were in Lebanon to help quell the violence and restore peace, as well as to support Israel, a Western ally. The attacks were eventually

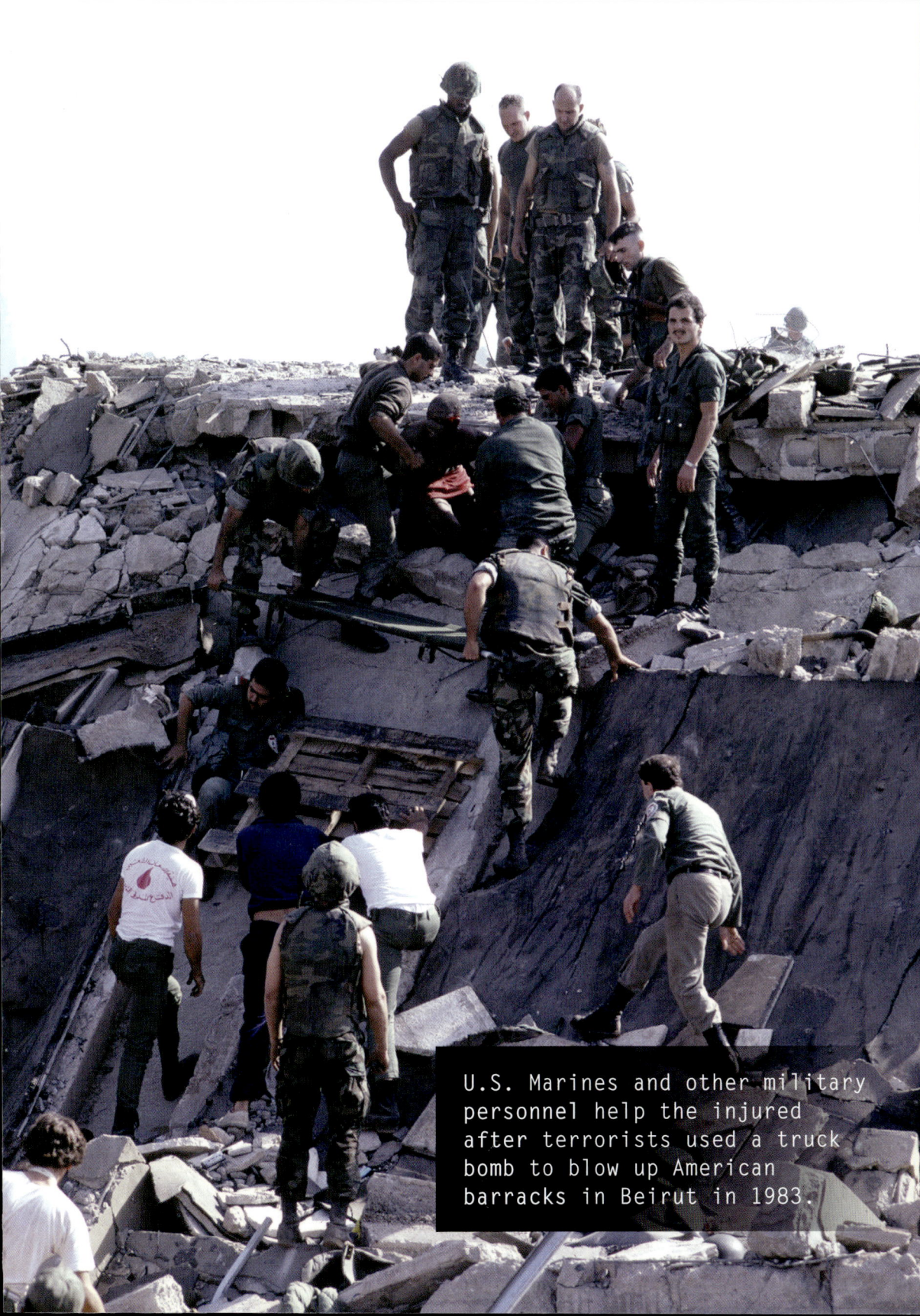

U.S. Marines and other military personnel help the injured after terrorists used a truck bomb to blow up American barracks in Beirut in 1983.

ISRAEL AND PALESTINE

The conflict between Israel and Palestine has been characterized by decades of violence between Jewish Israelis and Arab-Muslim Palestinians. Both groups view the region as their holy land. In 1948, the **United Nations (UN)** split the region between Israelis and Palestinians; however, Palestine wants control of areas in Israel called the West Bank (which includes Jerusalem) and the Gaza Strip. Jerusalem has been the site of many clashes between the two groups. Israel, a democracy, has had a close relationship with Western democracies such as the U.S. and Great Britain, thus drawing them into the conflict.

linked to Hezbollah, an Islamic political group known to use terror and violence to express its anti-Israeli and anti-Western beliefs. After the attacks, the U.S. initially pledged that it would not be intimidated by terrorism and that its policies and presence in Lebanon would remain unchanged. However, in February 1984, U.S. president Ronald Reagan ordered American troops to begin withdrawing from the area.

The Beirut barracks bombings had two powerful and lasting effects on the future of terrorism. As one of the first major suicide bomb attacks, it showcased to other terrorist groups the effectiveness of the suicide bomb. Additionally, America's withdrawal from Lebanon allowed the terrorists to claim success in their effort to remove the Western presence. Osama bin Laden, a wealthy Saudi Arabian who would later become the world's most infamous terrorist, stated in 1992 that the U.S.'s response to the attack had shown "the decline of American power and the weakness of the American soldier."

Bin Laden drew inspiration from the Beirut bombings and sought to use the same methods against Western nations in the years that followed. Bin Laden had taken part in the Muslim resistance to the Soviet Union when Soviet troops occupied the country of Afghanistan from 1979 to 1989. In late 1988, bin Laden and his friend Abdullah Azzam founded al Qaeda, an organization dedicated to forcefully removing non-Muslim influence from the Middle East. Bin Laden believed that employing terrorist tactics against

President Ronald Reagan and First Lady Nancy attend a memorial service for the servicemen killed in the 1983 Beirut barracks bombing.

non-Muslim civilians, including suicide bombs such as those used in Beirut, would help al Qaeda achieve its goals, but Azzam was opposed to such wide bloodshed, believing that the Islamic faith prohibited violence against women and children. The difference was nullified when Azzam was killed in a bomb attack in 1989, and bin Laden became the unchallenged leader of al Qaeda.

Throughout the 1990s, al Qaeda devoted itself to attacking the U.S. both

Ayman al-Zawahiri (left) and Osama bin Laden

within America and abroad. Based for a time in Saudi Arabia and then in Sudan, the group finally found refuge in Afghanistan in 1996, after an Islamic **extremist** political group called the Taliban took power. Under the protection of the Taliban, bin Laden found the mountainous and sparsely populated countryside of Afghanistan to be an ideal spot to establish and operate training camps for al Qaeda militants.

On February 23, 1998, al Qaeda announced itself as a serious threat when it published a declaration of war against the

U.S. and its allies. Bin Laden, Ayman al-Zawahiri, and three other Islamic leaders issued a **fatwa** against the West. The fatwa stated that American troops had been occupying Muslim lands, such as Jerusalem and Saudi Arabia, for more than seven years and accused them of humiliating and terrorizing Muslim people and plundering the countries' riches. These alleged acts were, in bin Laden's words, a "clear declaration of war on God, his messenger, and Muslims." The fatwa went on to declare that "the ruling to kill Americans and their allies, civilians and military, is an individual duty for every Muslim who can do it in any country in which it is possible to do it." These words should have sent a chill down the backs of Americans, but bin Laden's fatwa was not widely publicized and therefore went largely ignored.

The counterterrorism unit of America's Central Intelligence Agency (CIA) had been tracking bin Laden since 1996, and in May 1998, the CIA received information about his location and al Qaeda's goals and plans. The CIA began developing a strategy to capture bin Laden at one of his compounds, but concerns about civilian casualties

AYMAN AL-ZAWAHIRI

Ayman al-Zawahiri was the leader of an Islamist **jihad** group before becoming a prominent member of al Qaeda around 1998. Al-Zawahiri was considered to be the brains behind many al Qaeda operations. According to the U.S. State Department, he was the "strategic and operational planner" of the group, and he elevated his profile by releasing 12 videos of himself promoting al Qaeda's beliefs in 2008. Al-Zawahiri was believed to be hiding along the Afghan-Pakistan border, although numerous air strikes in the region intended to kill or capture him had failed as of 2011.

CENTRAL INTELLIGENCE AGENCY

The Central Intelligence Agency (CIA) is an agency within the U.S. federal government devoted to national security. The primary role of the CIA is to obtain and investigate information about foreign governments or individuals and determine possible threats to the U.S. Since 2001, the CIA's main objective has been to work closely with foreign governments to root out terrorists. Operatives, or spies, within the CIA also carry out covert missions at the request of the president.

Hijacked United Airlines Flight 175 approaches the World Trade Center's South Tower; 56 minutes after impact, the skyscraper would collapse.

and the high cost of the operation kept the plan from being carried out. This, in hindsight, was a huge mistake, as it may have prevented the greatest terrorist attack ever to occur on U.S. soil.

On September 11, 2001, hijackers seized control of four U.S. commercial airliners. They flew two planes into New York City's World Trade Center towers, causing the enormous buildings to collapse. A third plane crashed into the Pentagon, headquarters of the Department of Defense near Washington, D.C., and the fourth crashed in a Pennsylvania field after passengers fought against the hijackers. In all, the 9/11 attacks killed nearly 3,000 people.

People throughout the world were stunned that the U.S., one of the world's superpowers, had been attacked so blatantly and brutally. Many countries' leaders offered their condolences and support. Tony Blair, the British prime minister, stated that "the target of the terrorists was not only New York and Washington but the very values of freedom, tolerance, and decency which underpin our way

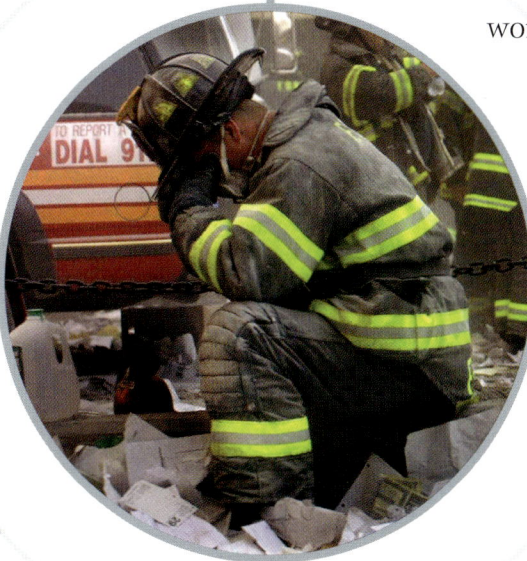

A New York firefighter on 9/11

of life." Immediately following the attacks, U.S. president George W. Bush and his administration speculated that the terrorists were likely affiliated with al Qaeda. In a speech to the nation, Bush pledged to bring the perpetrators to justice, making "no distinction between the terrorists who committed these acts and those who harbor them." On September 13, U.S. **secretary of state** Colin Powell named bin Laden the prime suspect in the planning of the attacks. The Bush administration called on the Taliban to hand over bin Laden or face invasion.

The Taliban refused to turn in bin Laden, and by the end of September, U.S. Special Forces were secretly operating inside Afghanistan to track down al Qaeda and its leaders. On October 7, a military mission called Operation Enduring Freedom began. The U.S. and its closest ally, Britain, commenced bombing Taliban and al Qaeda targets throughout Afghanistan. The War on Terror had truly begun.

Within weeks of 9/11, aircraft carriers and assault ships were carrying U.S. sailors, Marines, and combat aircraft toward Afghanistan.

THE TALIBAN

The Taliban is a Sunni Islamic extremist group that formed in the late 1980s to fight the Soviet occupation of Afghanistan. Although initially supported by the U.S., the Taliban proved to be an oppressive **regime** when it gained control of Afghanistan in 1996. The Taliban—which embraced an extremely conservative view of Islam—enforced rigid rules upon Afghanis, banning dance, music, and television, and it forbade women to be educated or employed. It also provided a haven in Afghanistan for terrorist groups such as al Qaeda. In 2001, the Taliban government was toppled after U.S.-led forces invaded the country.

CHAPTER TWO

WIDENING THE WAR

In October 2001, in an effort to find and prosecute terrorists who might have been living inside America, the U.S. passed the Uniting and Strengthening America by Providing Appropriate Tools Required to Intercept and Obstruct Terrorism Act, also known as the USA PATRIOT Act. The law gave the federal government the authority to search computer, financial, and medical records of suspected terrorists and to detain or **deport** immigrants who had ties to terrorists.

Although the act was supported by both Republican and Democratic members of the U.S. Congress, it was not without controversy. Critics of the law argued that the Patriot Act infringed on the **civil liberties**

of U.S. citizens and further stated that the definitions of "terrorism" and "terrorist ties" were ambiguous—under the law, any citizen could be searched for an activity as innocent as checking out a book on terrorism from a local library.

The passage of the Patriot Act brought the war against terrorism home for U.S. citizens. Many Americans, in the aftermath of 9/11, were willing to give up some of their freedoms if it meant greater security against more terrorist attacks. Supporters of the Patriot Act contended that the law was vital, as it allowed for covert investigation of potential terrorists. University of Chicago law professors Eric Posner and John Yoo wrote in support of the act, asserting that "civil liberties throughout our history have always expanded in peacetime and contracted during emergencies."

By the end of 2001, U.S.-led forces had toppled the Taliban regime in Afghanistan, but Osama bin Laden had yet to be captured. In his State of the Union address on January 29, 2002, President Bush focused on the war, stating that the nation's first goal was to eliminate individual terrorists and terrorist groups. He went on to state a second goal: to prevent terror-sponsoring regimes from threatening America and its allies with **weapons of mass destruction**

(WMD). He cited the governments of three countries—Iraq, Iran, and North Korea—as constituting an "Axis of Evil" that threatened world peace, inferring that these countries may provide weapons to terrorists or attack the U.S. or its allies.

Bush's Axis of Evil speech caused a stir both in the U.S. and abroad. The three countries he named, while known for their oppressive governments and long having been suspected of developing WMD,

President Bush addresses reporters about the Patriot Act

French helicopters land on an aircraft carrier during the Persian Gulf War; 34 countries in all sent combat troops and equipment to oppose Iraq.

had no clear ties to al Qaeda. The Bush administration might have believed at the time that these countries would sell weapons to terrorists, but, as would later be established, no hard evidence supported such a claim. Some critics even suggested that the Bush administration may have had another self-serving goal: to gain control, under the guise of the War on Terror, over such oil-rich regions as Iraq.

Following the speech, some of America's Western allies, such as Germany and France, which had initially supported the War on Terror and the invasion of Afghanistan, expressed concern that the U.S. was veering off track and losing sight of its original focus—dismantling al Qaeda and capturing or killing bin Laden. Many people remembered the Persian Gulf War of 1990–91, fought under president George H. W. Bush, and some wondered if the current president was using terrorism as an excuse to oust his father's old enemy, Iraqi president Saddam Hussein. In the Middle East, anti-American sentiments began to escalate among civilians. In Tehran, Iran, thousands of Iranians marched in protest of Bush's words, shouting "Death to America!"

THE PERSIAN GULF WAR

In August 1990, Iraqi troops, under the order of president Saddam Hussein, invaded the neighboring country of Kuwait on the grounds that Kuwait had historically been a territory of Iraq; however, the invasion also seemed motivated by Hussein's desire to gain control of the country's oil fields. When Hussein refused to pull out of Kuwait, the U.S. and 34 other nations formed a **coalition** to halt the invasion and liberate Kuwait. The coalition launched air strikes in January 1991, and a ground offensive in late February quickly caused Iraqi forces to retreat.

Around the world, critics of the speech feared that Bush's words would cause severe setbacks in foreign relations with the countries named and could even cause these regimes to increase their development of weapons in preparation for a possible attack by the U.S. or other Western forces. However, the Bush administration defended the speech, countering that these governments represented a strong threat to the world and, because previous negotiations with the countries' leaders to stop the oppression of their people had not worked, a publicly assertive tone was necessary to illuminate the repressive and threatening nature of their regimes.

The Axis of Evil speech was an indicator that the War on Terror was widening in scope, and in September 2002, Bush addressed the UN, arguing that Iraq had violated several international laws by harboring terrorists, engaging in human rights violations, and allegedly developing WMD—despite having been banned from possessing WMD since the end of the Gulf War. The **UN Security Council** passed a resolution that called for Iraq to permit weapons inspectors into the country and to cooperate fully. After the inspectors did not find

Iraqi schoolchildren praise president Saddam Hussein in September 2002, six months before he fell from power.

THE BUSH DOCTRINE

The Bush Doctrine describes president George W. Bush's policies on terror and foreign relations. If the U.S. was to defeat terrorism, Bush stated, it must take preemptive action—strike out against perceived threats before they could be carried out. Preemptive action, however, is forbidden by the UN, which permits military action only when a country has been invaded or with UN approval. The Bush Doctrine further asserted that the U.S. should support and defend democracy and that spreading democracy was a major step in combating terrorism.

SADDAM HUSSEIN

Saddam Hussein became vice president of Iraq in 1968 after the **secular** Ba'ath Party overthrew the government, and in 1979, he took control of the country by forcing the president's resignation. Hussein's leadership was characterized by his buildup of the Iraqi military (which became the strongest in the Middle East), his initiation of the Iran-Iraq War (1980–88), his 1990 invasion of Kuwait, and his oppression of the Shiites and **genocide** of the Kurdish people, an ethnic group that made up about 17 percent of Iraq's population. He was overthrown in 2003 and executed in 2006.

WMD, the U.S. set a deadline of March 17, 2003, for Hussein to hand over the alleged weapons—which many believed had been hidden—or face invasion.

Hussein expressed defiance to the deadline, and on March 19, 2003, the U.S. invaded, supported by coalition forces from Britain, Australia, Denmark, Poland, and Spain. Bombs were dropped and missiles fired on the capital city of Baghdad, and ground forces in Kuwait crossed the border into Iraq. Bush announced that the goals were clear: "Iraq will be disarmed, the Iraqi regime will be ended, and the long-suffering Iraqi people will be free." With this statement, it became evident that the War on Terror had become, at least in part, a war for democracy.

Around the world, millions of people protested the invasion; even many Americans voiced their strong objections. Russian president Vladimir Putin called for a halt of the invasion, and French president Jacques Chirac warned that the Iraq War would have dire consequences. The international unity that had developed after 9/11 was rapidly dissolving.

South Koreans protest the Iraq War in September 2003; the U.S. had asked South Korea and many other countries to send support troops.

Hussein went into hiding as his over-matched army fought against the invading forces and soon fell. In December 2003, Hussein was captured; he would be executed three years later. Evidence of the alleged WMD was never found, embarrassing the Bush administration. Worse, Iraq, which had not previously been proven to have ties to al Qaeda, suddenly became a haven for terrorists due to instability within the country, and violence erupted between two Islamic **sects**, the Sunnis and Shiites. Another negative consequence of the invasion was that now, an increasing number of Muslims around the world began to feel that perhaps al Qaeda had been right: maybe the U.S. and its allies—having invaded two Middle Eastern countries—truly were targeting the Islamic faith.

With electrical power having been knocked out in Baghdad, an Iraqi family eats their supper by lantern light in December 2003.

SUNNI AND SHIA IN IRAQ

The majority of Iraq's population consists of two Muslim sects: Sunni and Shia. The split occurred after the death of Islam's founder, Muhammad, in A.D. 632. Shiites believed that the religion's new leader should be someone from the prophet's family; Sunnis believed he should be elected based on his ability. During Saddam Hussein's rule, Sunni leaders comprised much of the government, despite the fact that more than 60 percent of the country was Shiite. After Hussein's fall, Iraq held elections that placed many Shiites in leadership roles, angering the Sunni people.

THE CONFLICT ESCALATES

On May 1, 2003, President Bush, in a televised speech to the U.S. Navy, declared that major combat operations in Iraq had come to an end. Behind him, splayed across the aircraft carrier USS *Abraham Lincoln*, was a banner that read "Mission Accomplished." Bush stated that U.S.-led coalition forces had prevailed in Iraq, although he went on to say that "our mission continues. Al Qaeda is wounded, not destroyed." The same day, U.S. defense secretary Donald Rumsfeld announced that major combat operations in Afghanistan had ended, and that 8,000 of the 11,000 U.S. troops who remained in the country were turning their focus to stabilizing and rebuilding Afghanistan.

Bush's and Rumsfeld's words were met with criticism, especially as the number of U.S. and coalition casualties increased in the weeks and months that

An anti-Bush poster

President Bush announces the end of major combat operations in Iraq—an infamous moment in May 2003.

MISSION ACCOMPLISHED

The White House initially defended President Bush's remarks upon the USS *Abraham Lincoln* in May 2003, stating that the banner represented only the mission of that particular aircraft carrier and not of the overall operation, although Bush later conceded that the banner was misleading to the American people. White House officials, clarifying Rumsfeld's remarks about operations ending in Afghanistan, stated that the administration wanted to send a message that major combat in Afghanistan was over so that other countries would be more willing to send troops for peacekeeping and rebuilding efforts.

followed. People worldwide viewed the "Mission Accomplished" banner as a declaration that the Iraq War had ended; however, fierce fighting continued there, and in the months following Bush's speech, more than half of the troops stationed in Afghanistan were transferred to Iraq. The Iraq conflict appeared far from over. Rather, critics stated, the Iraq War was using up resources that should have been used in the hunt for bin Laden and the fight against terrorists. In the summer of 2003, about 11,000 U.S. troops were stationed in Afghanistan, in contrast to 135,000 in Iraq.

As Western military **occupation** of Afghanistan and Iraq continued, the War on Terror persisted on homefronts as well. Allied governments continued their efforts to thwart terrorist attacks, yet two major attacks—one in Madrid, Spain, and another in London, England—called into question the effectiveness of the allies' intelligence operations. On March 11, 2004, bombs exploded on four commuter trains in Madrid, just days before the country's general elections. Ten bombs had been carried onto the trains in the backpacks of terrorists. The explosions left 191 dead and more than 1,800 wounded. The bombing was linked to Islamic extremists, and though no direct ties were found between the attackers and al Qaeda, a message from an al Qaeda leader stated that the group was "proud" of the bombings. Days later, Spain's Socialist Party, which had pledged to withdraw troops from Iraq, was elected to power. As it

The Madrid bombings of March 2004 might have been even deadlier, as 13 bombs were planted on 4 trains but only 10 detonated.

AL QAEDA IN IRAQ

In 2004, a strong al Qaeda presence in Iraq began to emerge. Led by Abu Musab al-Zarqawi, a Jordanian militant who moved into the country after the 2001 Afghanistan invasion, the group al Qaeda in Iraq (AQI) joined the Sunni-led **insurgency**, using terrorist tactics such as suicide bombs, kidnappings, and executions in its fight against the occupying Western forces and the new Iraqi government. AQI began losing popularity after its violence killed many Iraqi civilians and after al-Zarqawi was killed in 2006, but the group regained strength in late 2009.

A suicide bomber destroyed this double-decker London bus nearly an hour after bombs went off in underground trains on July 7, 2005.

had promised, the ruling party withdrew Spanish troops. On April 15, bin Laden released a videotape promising that al Qaeda would not mount operations against countries that did not attack Muslims. Al Qaeda seemed to view the Madrid attacks as a victory.

The following year, on July 7, 2005, four suicide bombers blew themselves up in London, three on the city's underground trains and one on a double-decker bus. Fifty-six people were killed, including the terrorists, and more than 700 people were injured. The four bombers were Islamic extremists; however, each was a British citizen with no known criminal record. In a videotape found months later, one of the bombers described his reasons for the terrorist attack, stating, "What you have witnessed now is only the beginning of a string of attacks that will continue and become stronger until you pull your forces out of Afghanistan and Iraq. And until you stop your financial and military support to America and Israel." The videotape had been edited to include words from al Qaeda mastermind Ayman al-Zawahiri, intending to draw a link between the London bombings and al Qaeda, though no connection was ever proven.

The London bombings showed a new face of terrorism. Whereas the 2001 attacks in the U.S. and the 2004 attacks in Madrid had been carried out by non-citizens of those countries, the perpetrators of the 2005 London attacks were British. The Madrid and London attacks raised questions as to whether the War on Terror was working or if it was instead increasing the hatred and reach of Islamic extremists. In April 2006, CIA director general Michael Hayden warned that "new jihadist networks and cells, sometimes united by little more than their anti-Western agendas, are increasingly likely to emerge" in opposition to Western presence in Iraq, thus increasing the threat of attacks worldwide.

In Iraq, even though a tenuous democratic government was in place, the war raged on with no clear end in sight. Although the old Iraqi military was long-vanquished, an insurgency against Western occupation of the country was in full force, and the American people were growing increasingly critical of the Bush Doctrine. Allegations of torture in the Abu Ghraib prison also cast U.S. forces in a bad light. In America's 2006 general elections, Democrats gained control of the U.S. Congress, which seemed to indicate that Americans were dissatisfied with the way the Republican-controlled Congress and the Bush administration were handling the war. By the end of 2006, total coalition military deaths in Iraq numbered more than 3,200. It was clear that a new approach was necessary.

General George Casey, the top U.S. commander in Iraq, urged Bush to begin

A hooded anti-war activist simulates a scene of torture in front of the U.S. Supreme Court building in reaction to the Abu Ghraib prison scandal.

ABU GHRAIB

After the 2003 Iraq invasion, many prisoners of war were held by the U.S. in the Abu Ghraib prison outside Baghdad. In 2004, photos released to the public revealed incidents of abuse and torture carried out by some U.S. Army guards upon Iraqi prisoners, including various humiliations and physical and sexual abuse. Eleven soldiers were convicted; some were sentenced to jail, but others were released with only a fine. The Abu Ghraib scandal caused many people around the world to question the U.S.'s motives and attitude toward Iraq.

The 2007 troop surge meant that more combat troops, like these U.S. Army soldiers, patrolled the streets of Baghdad alongside Iraqi civilians.

pulling U.S. troops out of major cities and to focus on training soldiers and police within the new Iraqi government to keep order. However, other experts, including retired Army General Jack Keane, urged for an escalation of troops—a "surge" that would push the insurgents out of Baghdad as well as root out al Qaeda operatives hidden in the countryside. Bush, despite opposition from some members of his own administration, adopted the plan. In January 2007, he announced his intention to send more troops in a strategy he called "The New Way Forward," also known simply as "the surge." The president called for the deployment of some 20,000 additional U.S. troops to Iraq, many of them to the Baghdad area, and lengthened the tours of 4,000 Marines.

Before the surge, in Anbar, a large province in western Iraq, al Qaeda had been attacking Sunni Muslims, including women and children. The Sunnis, who had been engaged in a wide-scale insurgency against coalition forces and the new Iraqi government, now turned to the Americans for help against their al Qaeda attackers. Because of the surge, there were now enough troops to pacify the Anbar province, and violence there ebbed. In Baghdad, too, the surge seemed to quell the bloodshed, although many people were skeptical about how long the relative peace would last. The initial success of the surge did not come without a cost: the U.S. and its coalition partners suffered 901 fatalities in 2007, making it the deadliest year of the war since 2004.

CHAPTER FOUR

A SHIFT IN APPROACH

As Bush's eight years as president drew to a close, the world's attention turned to the 2008 U.S. presidential election. The Republican Party had nominated Senator John McCain as its candidate, and the Democratic Party had nominated Senator Barack Obama. The War on Terror was a major issue in both campaigns, and the two candidates held differing views. McCain had been a supporter of the initial invasion of Iraq and the 2007 surge, whereas Obama had opposed both. Obama pledged to bring U.S. troops home from Iraq in an 18-month phased withdrawal; McCain was against setting a timetable, stating that withdrawing from the country before it could govern itself peaceably would lead only to more problems. On Afghanistan, both candidates agreed that more troops needed to be sent to the country—where al Qaeda elements still operated and the Taliban was regrouping—with increased focus upon fortifying the Afghan-Pakistan border.

The entire world anticipated the outcome of the election, knowing that a new U.S. president could profoundly impact the wars in Iraq and Afghanistan. Obama won the most votes, seemingly due in part to his pledge to withdraw troops from Iraq. One of the first steps Obama took as president was to call for an end to the phrase "War on Terror." Instead, he referred to the conflict

Barack Obama visited Israel during his presidential campaign in July 2008, underscoring his promise to work for peace in the Middle East.

AMERICAN-MUSLIM RELATIONS

One of Barack Obama's stated goals upon becoming president was to repair America's image among Muslims. Many people believed that the aggressive and often unilateral actions of the Bush administration had created a rift between Americans and people of Islamic faith. Obama aimed to prove to the Muslim world that the ongoing struggle was not a war against the Islamic religion but rather against extremist groups who perpetrate attacks in the name of a fundamentalist version of Islam. In 2009, Obama traveled to the Middle East in an effort to spread this message.

THE OPIUM TRADE

Afghanistan is the world's largest producer of opium, which comes from poppies and is an ingredient in heroin, an illegal and habit-forming drug. Since the 2001 fall of the Taliban, which prohibited farmers from growing opium, production of the crop in Afghanistan has been on the rise. The ongoing war and widespread poverty has led many farmers who had been growing food crops such as wheat and rice to revert to opium, which is a more lucrative crop. Ironically, warlords engaged in drug trafficking used their proceeds to fund the Taliban resurgence.

An Afghan boy works in a poppy field in the Tora Bora region of eastern Afghanistan in May 2002.

as the Overseas Contingency Operation. The War on Terror was associated with the Bush administration, and Obama aimed to under-score that he would take a different approach to the conflict. He stated that he would seek to build a new relationship between the U.S. and Muslims around the world, "one based upon mutual interest and mutual respect; and one based upon the truth that America and Islam are not exclusive, and need not be in competition."

One of Obama's campaign promises was to shift the focus of the war back to Afghanistan—where the conflict had start-ed—rather than Iraq. Although there was an al Qaeda presence in Iraq, the hub of the terrorist network remained in Afghanistan, primarily in the mountains along its border

with Pakistan, where bin Laden was believed to be hiding. Adding to the terrorist problem was the Taliban, which had been regaining strength since its initial fall and had teamed up with al Qaeda to wage steady attacks against U.S. and North Atlantic Treaty Organization (NATO) forces in Afghanistan. The Taliban's resurgence could be credited in part to Afghanistan's illegal opium trade, which helped fund the group, as well as to the haven the group had found in Pakistan.

The Pakistani government did not sym-pathize with the Taliban or condone Islamic terrorism, and initially it had seemed will-ing to cooperate with the U.S. in its War on Terror; however, funds that were provided to Pakistan by the U.S. to aid in ousting the Taliban were often misused, leading the U.S.

to question Pakistan's commitment to fighting insurgents and terrorists. Heightening the danger was the fact that Pakistan had a **nuclear weapons** program, and a possible Taliban rise to power could give the insurgents, and perhaps al Qaeda, access to WMD. As U.S. relations with Pakistan grew tense, the Obama administration worked to strengthen its alliance with the country by holding diplomatic talks and offering monetary support. Military and political experts agreed that having Pakistan fully committed to fighting terrorists would be a critical step in winning the War on Terror.

Obama analyzed strategies to combat the Taliban insurgency and root out al Qaeda terrorists in Afghanistan. In March 2009, the president announced the deployment of 17,000 additional troops to help secure the region, train Afghani forces, and provide security in advance of the country's upcoming presidential election. In December 2009, Obama announced his decision to send 30,000 more troops to Afghanistan, promising that after 18 months, the troops would begin to withdraw. The decision to send more troops into battle was unpopular with many Americans who had voted for him based on his promise to end the war on both fronts, but Obama defended the action, stating that a surge in troops would help bring the war to a more successful close.

The 2009 presidential election in the new democratic government of Afghanistan was plagued by corruption and turmoil. Election-day violence and fraud (consisting

KABUL UN ATTACK

On October 28, 2009, insurgents disguised in police uniforms stormed the UN guesthouse in Kabul, Afghanistan. Twelve people, including six UN employees, were killed. The Taliban claimed responsibility, stating that the attacks were in protest of the upcoming elections in Afghanistan. One American was killed in the attacks; that, plus two helicopter crashes earlier in the week, made October 2009 the deadliest month for Americans in Afghanistan since the war began in 2001. The UN declared it would be undeterred by the attacks, and elections were held as scheduled.

The UN guesthouse in Kabul, Afghanistan, was ravaged when the Taliban attacked with gunfire, grenades, and bombs in October 2009.

Hamid Karzai (right), as the appointed but not yet elected leader of Afghanistan, casts his vote during the 2004 presidential election in Kabul.

of such problems as bribery, multiple-voter registration, and the selling of voting cards) marred the outcome of the August 20 election, and a do-over was scheduled for November. However, just days before the election, Abdullah Abdullah, the opponent to **incumbent** president Hamid Karzai, withdrew from the race, and Karzai was declared the winner. President Obama then urged Karzai to crack down on the corruption—reportedly including bribery and drug trafficking—present within his government. Obama believed that having a strong and fair democratic government was the key to stabilizing Afghanistan, halting insurgent violence, and allowing the occupying forces to eventually hand over control of the country to the Afghanis. Until such a government was in place, Western leaders agreed, U.S. and NATO forces would need to remain in the country.

Although Obama had shifted the military's attention to Afghanistan, the conflict was not yet over in Iraq. By August 2009, all coalition countries except the U.S. had withdrawn their troops from Iraq. Obama followed through on his promise to withdraw U.S. combat forces by August 2010, with approximately 50,000

HAMID KARZAI

After the Taliban government was toppled, Hamid Karzai, a former leader of an anti-Taliban movement, became prominent in Afghanistan's government, and he was elected president in 2004, when the country held its first democratic presidential election since the fall of the Taliban. Due to his stance against terrorism and the Taliban, his presidency was supported by the U.S. However, his failure to crack down on the illegal drug trade and allegations of bribery and other corruption within his government created tension between Karzai and the Western world by 2010.

troops then remaining in the country to train Iraqi forces and provide intelligence. Then, in the predawn hours of May 2, 2011, the U.S. shifted its attention to Pakistan in a headline-making way. Having tracked the long-elusive bin Laden to a compound in the northern city of Abbottabad, the U.S. sent in several helicopters carrying a team of Navy SEALs. The SEALs swept through the compound, and bin Laden and three al Qaeda members were shot and killed, marking the raid as one of the most pivotal moments yet in the war.

From military campaigns to diplomacy, and homefront legislation to global alliances, the War on Terror has proven to be a struggle with many facets. It has proven, too, to be a most difficult dilemma to sort out, especially as its end goals have come to include not only the defeat of increasingly scattered terrorist groups but also the spread of democracy in the Middle East and improved communication with nations at odds with the U.S. and the West. Resolving such a complex problem is the challenge that President Obama and other leaders will face in the months and years to come.

Iraqi anti-terrorism forces assumed peacekeeping responsibilities after the U.S. withdrew the last of its combat troops in August 2010.

NATO

NATO is an alliance among 28 countries in North America and Europe; the organization uses military or political support to protect the freedom and security of its member countries. After the 9/11 terrorist attacks on America, NATO launched operations against terrorism, such as sending naval ships to patrol the Mediterranean Sea and committing troops to Afghanistan. NATO has not been officially involved in the Iraq War, although some of its member countries have sent their own troops.

civil liberties — individual rights and freedoms guaranteed by the U.S. Constitution, such as the freedom of speech, freedom of religion, and freedom from unwarranted searches and seizures

coalition — an alliance of individuals or groups who join together for a common cause

democracy — a form of government in which the leaders are elected by the people; the term also refers to social equality of the individuals in society

deport — to send out of the country; in many immigration cases, to deport means to send the immigrants back to their home countries

diplomatic — describing a way of negotiating or interacting without arousing hostility

extremist — describing someone who holds views that are radical or far from the traditional or common view

fatwa — a binding edict, or order, given by an Islamic religious leader; Osama bin Laden's 1998 fatwa against the West was not a fatwa in the truest sense, as he did not meet the qualifications for a religious leader

genocide — the deliberate extermination or destruction of a group of people based on their ethnicity, culture, or political beliefs

incumbent — currently holding an indicated position, role, or office

insurgency — a revolt or uprising against a government or ruling force

jihad — a holy war waged by Muslims as a religious duty against people who do not believe in Islam

militants — people who use aggression or combat in support of a cause

nuclear weapons — bombs or missiles with enormous destructive power derived from the uncontrolled splitting or combining of atoms

occupation — the holding and control of an area by a foreign military or force

regime — a government in power or prevailing system of government; the term often has a negative and oppressive implication

secretary of state — the U.S. president's chief foreign affairs adviser, who often meets with leaders and ambassadors of other countries for diplomatic talks and negotiations

sects — groups within a larger group that adhere to distinctive doctrines or beliefs

secular — being void of religious ties or affiliations

United Nations (UN) — an organization with representatives from 192 nations that deals with international law, human rights, and economic progress, and aims to maintain peace between nations through communication

UN Security Council — a body of the UN composed of representatives from 15 countries; the Security Council can pass resolutions that authorize war or impose economic penalties upon countries

weapons of mass destruction (WMD) — weapons such as nuclear bombs and chemicals or gases that are capable of killing large numbers of people or destroying huge areas

ENDNOTES

SELECTED BIBLIOGRAPHY

Honigsberg, Peter Jan. *Our Nation Unhinged: The Human Consequences of the War on Terror*. Berkeley, Calif.: University of California Press, 2009.

Kepel, Gilles, and Jean-Pierre Milleli, eds. Translated by Pascale Ghazaleh. *Al Qaeda in Its Own Words*. Cambridge, Mass.: Belknap Press of Harvard University Press, 2008.

Public Broadcasting Service. "The Online News Hour: Afghanistan and the War on Terror Political Timeline." PBS. http://www.pbs.org/newshour/indepth_coverage/asia/afghanistan/timeline/timeline8.html.

Riedel, Bruce. *The Search for al Qaeda: Its Leadership, Ideology, and Future*. Washington, D.C.: Brookings Institution Press, 2008.

Rubin, Barry, and Judith Colp Rubin. *Chronologies of Modern Terrorism*. Armonk, N.Y.: M. E. Sharpe, 2008.

Sciutto, Jim. *Against Us: The New Face of America's Enemies in the Muslim World*. New York: Harmony Books, 2008.

Tyler, Patrick. *A World of Trouble: The White House and the Middle East—From the Cold War to the War on Terror*. New York: Farrar, Straus and Giroux, 2009.

U.S. Department of Defense. "U.S. Department of Defense Official News Website." http://www.defenselink.mil/.